Common Core Math Grade 3 Practice Test

Author: Bright Minds Publishing.

Common Core State Standards ® Introduction & Curriculum

The Common Core State Standards provide a consistent, clear curriculum about what students are expected to learn, so teachers and parents know what they need to do to help. Various states and school districts offer tests that measure student proficiency. These practice tests are based on the Common Core Standards curriculum at http://www.corestandards.org/

Common Core Standard committee (or its affiliates) were not involved in the production of these tests, and they do not endorse these practice tests.

Bright Minds Publishing

Contents

1. How is seven thousand one hundred two written in standard form?

    A 7120

    B 7012

    C 7201

    D 7102

2. Which of the following is the same as 7203?

    A seven thousand twenty-three

    B seven thousand two hundred three

    C seven hundred twenty-three

    D seventy thousand two hundred three

3. Which set of numbers is in order from least to greatest?

    A 123,132,256,281

    B 256,281,123,132

    C 132,123,256,281

    D 281,256,132,123

4. Which number has a 3 in the ones place and a 3 in the tens place?

A 3113

B 3131

C 1133

D 1331

5. Which does 7 represent in the number below?

3847

A 7

B 70

C 700

D 7000

6. Which of these is nine hundred four?

A 94

B 9004

C 940

D 904

7. What is 517 rounded to the nearest ten?

    A 520

    B 510

    C 500

    D 600

8. Serena has 352 stickers in her sticker book. Which of these equal 352?

    A $3 + 5 + 2$

    B $3 + 50 + 200$

    C $300 + 50 + 2$

    D $300 + 50 + 20$

9. Which number is 7000 + 900 + 6 ?

    A 796

    B 7906

    C 7960

    D 7096

10. The rectangle below shows $\frac{1}{3}$ shaded.

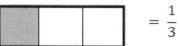

$= \frac{1}{3}$

What fractional part of a rectangle below is equal to $\frac{1}{3}$?

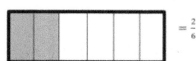

$= \frac{2}{6}$

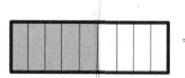

$= \frac{5}{9}$

A

C

$= \frac{4}{6}$

$= \frac{8}{9}$

B

D

11. $\frac{2}{6} + \frac{1}{6} =$

A $\frac{4}{6}$

B $\frac{2}{3}$

C $\frac{2}{6}$

D $\frac{1}{2}$

12. A cake was divided was divided into sixths. Joshua ate $\frac{3}{6}$ of the cake. Geri ate $\frac{1}{6}$ of the cake. Louis ate $\frac{2}{6}$ of the cake. How much of the cake was eaten?

A $\frac{1}{2}$

B 1 (whole cake)

C $\frac{5}{6}$

D $\frac{1}{2}$

12. A cake was divided was divided into sixths. Joshua ate $\frac{3}{6}$ of the cake. Geri ate $\frac{1}{6}$ of the cake. Louis ate $\frac{2}{6}$ of the cake. How much of the cake was eaten?

A $\frac{1}{2}$

B 1 (whole cake)

C $\frac{5}{6}$

D $\frac{1}{2}$

13. What is the difference?

$$\frac{4}{5} - \frac{3}{5} =$$

A $\frac{1}{5}$

B $\frac{2}{5}$

C $\frac{1}{2}$

D 1

14. Lily has $10.00 to buy an art set that costs $9.35. How much change should she get back?

    A $0.75

    B $0.70

    C $0.65

    D $0.62

15. Howard compared the prices of two headphones. The table below shows the prices.

Cost of Headphones

Brand	Cost
A	$14.56
B	$19.99

How much more does Brand B cost than Brand A?

    A $5.43

    B $5.54

    C $6.34

    D $6.43

16. McKenna bought 5 books for $5.50. How much did each book cost to buy?

    A $27.50

    B $10.75

    C $2.25

    D $1.10

17. Five children earned $25 for selling lemonade for an hour. They decided to divide the money equally. How much money did each of the children get?

    A $125.00

    B $30.00

    C $5.00

    D $2.50

18. Yasmin shaded $\frac{1}{2}$ of the figure.

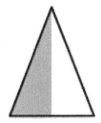

Which decimal equals $\frac{1}{2}$?

    A 0.05

    B 0.5

    C 0.55

    D 5.0

This space left blank intentionally

19. Look at the number sentence below.

$$74 + \square = 131$$

    A 57

    B 58

    C 67

    D 74

20. The town of Carney has 3707 grown-ups and 1291 children. How many people live in Carney?

    A 5098

    B 5008

    C 4998

    D 4988

This space left blank intentionally

21. The figure below is a model for a multiplication sentence.

$$6 \times 3 = 18$$

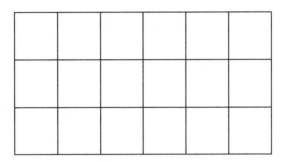

Which division sentence is modelled by the same figure?

    A $6 \div 3 = 2$

    B $12 \div 3 = 4$

    C $12 \div 6 = 2$

    D $18 \div 6 = 3$

22. Annie and Oliver each used a different number sentence to solve the same problem. Annie used this number sentence:

$$12 \times 7 = 84$$

Which of the following number sentences could Oliver have used?

    A $7 \div 84 = 12$

    B $84 \div 7 = 12$

    C $12 + 7 = 19$

    D $84 - 12 = 70$

23. There are 252 seats in the cafeteria. Each seat is full during the 4 lunches served during the day. How many people sit in the cafeteria during lunch?

    A 256

    B 504

    C 1008

    D 1016

24. How much is seven times five hundred sixty-four?

    A 3948

    B 3928

    C 3618

    D 3528

25. On Thursday, 1050 people went to the park. Four times as many people visited on Saturday than on Thursday. How many people visited the park on Saturday?

    A 1054

    B 2100

    C 3175

    D 4200

26. Daniel has 512 leaves in his leaf collection. He divides the leaves in four equal piles. How many leaves are in each pile?

    A 132

    B 128

    C 126

    D 114

27. A play had 5628 people attend during the three days it was performed with an equally divided amount of people attending each day. How many people attended the play each day?

    A 1862

    B 1876

    C 1914

    D 1938

28. What number can be multiplied with 4187 to give the answer 0?

$$4187 \times \square = 0$$

    A 4187

    B 100

    C 1

    D 0

29. Which number sentence is true?

A $642 \div 642 = 642 \times 1$

B $642 \div 1 = 642 \times 0$

C $642 \div 1 = 642 \times 1$

D $642 \div 0 = 642 \times 642$

30. Mrs. Hudson bought 7 candles. All the candles were the same price. The total cost was $63. How much money did each candle cost?

A $441

B $63

C $11

D $9

31. Thomas had $30. He paid $11 for a cap from his favorite basketball team. Then he went to buy a ticket to the game for $8. What amount of money did Thomas have then?

A $1

B $8

C $11

D $19

This space left blank intentionally

32. In one week, a truck driver drove 704 miles on Monday and 598 miles on Wednesday. If the truck driver drives the same number of miles 4 weeks in a row, how many miles does she drive in all?

    A 6309

    B 5208

    C 3414

    D 1310

33. Mr. Breslin bought 36 bottle waters packed equally into 3 containers. Which number sentence shows how to find the number of water bottles in each container?

    A $36 \div 3 = \square$

    B $36 \times 3 = \square$

    C $36 - 3 = \square$

    D $36 + 3 = \square$

34. If Shauna bought a package of strawberries for \$3.25 and she paid with a \$5 bill, which expression shows the correct amount of change?

    A $\$5 \times \$3.25 = \square$

    B $\$5 \div \$3.25 = \square$

    C $\$5 + \$3.25 = \square$

    D $\$5 - \$3.25 = \square$

35. Which statement shows four more than 10?

   A $4 - 10$

   B $4 + 10$

   C $4 \div 10$

   D 4×10

36. Which expression shows half of 12?

   A $12 - 2$

   B $12 + 2$

   C $12 \div 2$

   D 12×2

37. What number makes this number sentence true?

$$5 + 7 = \boxed{} \times 3$$

   A 2

   B 4

   C 5

   D 6

38. Which sign goes in the box to make the number sentence true?

$$8 \; \square \; 4 = 32$$

A ÷

B ×

C −

D +

39. Francesca practiced piano for 420 minutes in one week. How many hours did she practice?

A 42 hours

B 10 hours

C 8 hours

D 7 hours

40. If $4 \times 9 \times 10 = 360$, then what is $9 \times 4 \times 10$?

A 36

B 40

C 360

D 900

41. One bunch of grapes are on sale for $2.50, how much will 3 bunches cost?

A $5.00

B $7.50

C $10.00

D $12.50

42. How much will 2 oranges and 3 limes cost?

Prices	
Oranges	33¢
Limes	21¢

A $1.41

B $1.29

C $0.75

D $0.54

43. One marker cost $0.29. Two markers cost $0.58. Three markers cost $0.87. If the cost of each marker remains the same, how much would 4 markers cost?

A $1.16

B $1.21

C $3.48

D $6.96

44. Look at the linear pattern below.

$$6, 12, 18, 24, 30, \underline{\quad}$$

What comes next in this pattern?

    A 32

    B 36

    C 38

    D 40

45. Which is the BEST method to determine the length of a football field?

    A inches

    B feet

    C yards

    D miles

46. What is the area of this figure?

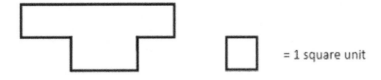

= 1 square unit

    A 4 square units

    B 2 square units

    C 10 square units

    D 7 square units

47. A rectangle is 5 inches long and 7 inches wide. What is the area of the rectangle?

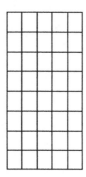

    A 25 square inches

    B 30 square inches

    C 35 square inches

    D 40 square inches

48. A kitchen in a house is shaped like a rectangle 4 meters long and 3 meters wide.

3 meters

4 meters

What is the perimeter in meters of the kitchen?

    A 12 meters

    B 14 meters

    C 16 meters

    D 20 meters

49. Look at the polygon below.

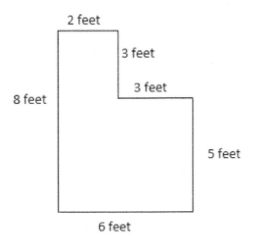

What is the perimeter of the polygon?

    A 27 feet

    B 25 feet

    C 23 feet

    D 21 feet

50. Each side of the parallelogram is 6 inches long.

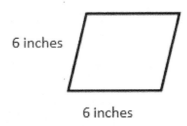

What is the perimeter in inches of the parallelogram?

    A 12 inches

    B 20 inches

    C 24 inches

    D 32 inches

51. How many inches are in 3 feet 2 inches?

     A 26 inches

     B 36 inches

     C 38 inches

     D 42 inches

52. Which of these is a pentagon?

         A   **C**

         B   **D**

53. The figure below is what shape?

     A pentagon

     B hexagon

     C octagon

     D diamond

54. Which of the following shapes is an octagon?

A

C

B

D

55. An equilateral triangle MUST have

    A 3 sides that are the same length.

    B 2 sides that are the same length.

    C one side that has the length of 3.

    D no sides that are the same length.

56. How many pairs of parallel sides does a parallelogram have?

    A 0

    B 1

    C 2

    D 3

57. Which shape has 4 right angles?

      A triangle

      B circle

      C parallelogram

      D rectangle

58. Look at the angles on the following shape.

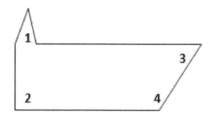

Which angle is a right angle?

      A 1

      B 2

      C 3

      D 4

This space left blank intentionally

59. Which object is a sphere?

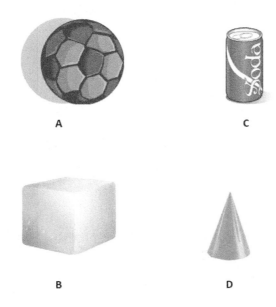

A

C

B

D

60. Which shapes make up this solid object?

A cone and cylinder

B cylinder and square

C cube and cylinder

D cube and circle

61. There are 14 marbles in a bag. There are 1 blue, 3 green, 4 red, and 7 yellow marbles. What color is MOST likely to be taken out of the bag next?

    A blue

    B green

    C red

    D yellow

62. A spinner landed on "Yellow" 5 times, "Blue" 2 times, and "Green" 6 times. Which tally chart shows these results?

Spin Results	
Yellow	||||
Blue	||
Green	|||

A

Spin Results	
Yellow	
Blue	|
Green	

C

Spin Results	
Yellow	
Blue	||
Green	|

B

Spin Results	
Yellow	
Blue	||
Green	

D

63. Simon asked his classmates to name their favorite kind of pizza. Two classmates liked sausage pizza, 10 classmates liked pepperoni pizza, and 11 classmates liked cheese pizza.

Which of the following shows Simon's information?

Favorite Pizza

Sausage	||
Pepperoni	ЖН ЖН
Cheese	ЖН ЖНI

A

Favorite Pizza

Sausage	ЖН ЖН
Pepperoni	||
Cheese	ЖН ЖНI

C

Favorite Pizza

Sausage	|||
Pepperoni	ЖН ЖН
Cheese	ЖН ЖН

B

Favorite Pizza

Sausage	ЖН
Pepperoni	ЖН ЖН
Cheese	ЖН |||

D

This space intentionally left blank

64. A group of children tossed a coin 12 times. The coin landed on heads 7 times and on tails 5 times. Which tally chart shows these tosses?

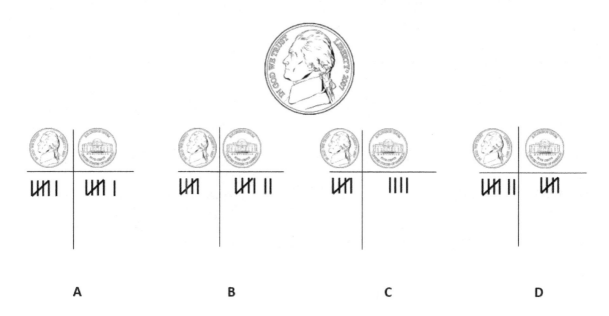

A   B   C   D

This space intentionally left blank

65. Alan, Jennifer, and Nicholas were tossing a coin to see how many times it would land on heads. They each tossed the coin 10 times and recorded their results with tally marks.

Coin Toss	
Name	**Heads**
Alan	卌
Jennifer	|||
Nicholas	卌 ||

Which graph shows their results?

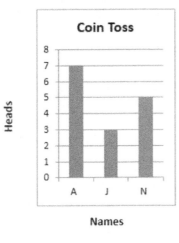

A

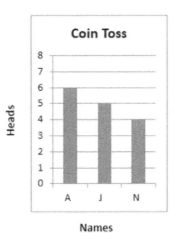

C

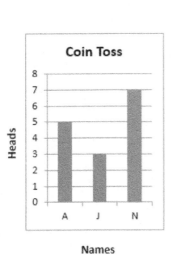

B

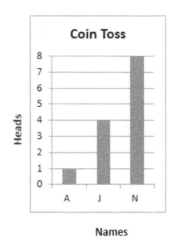

D

Grade 3 Math Questions: Section 2

1. How is five thousand, eighty-seven written in standard form?

A 5087

B 5870

C 5078

D 5780

2. Which of the following is the same as 5053?

A five hundred fifty-three

B fifty thousand five hundred three

C five thousand fifty-three

D five thousand five hundred three

3. Which set of numbers is in order from greatest to least?

A 145,154,217,293

B 217,154,145,293

C 154,145,293,217

D 293,217,154,145

4. Which number has a 7 in the hundreds place and a 7 in the thousands place?

    A 2774

    B 7742

    C 7472

    D 7247

5. Which digit is in the tens place in the number 9851?

    A 9

    B 8

    C 5

    D 1

6. Which number has the same digit in both the tens place and the thousands place?

    A 8518

    B 4364

    C 9227

    D 1015

7. What is 2129 rounded to the nearest hundred?

    A 2200

    B 2100

    C 2000

    D 3000

8. Bryan has 143 video games in his collection. Which of these equal 143?

    A $100 + 40 + 3$

    B $1 + 4 + 3$

    C $1 + 40 + 3$

    D $100 + 40 + 30$

9. Which number means $2000 + 10 + 8$?

    A 218

    B 281

    C 2018

    D 2108

10. The square shows $\frac{1}{2}$ shaded.

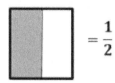 $= \frac{1}{2}$

What fractional part of a square below is equal to $\frac{1}{2}$?

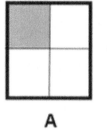 $= \frac{1}{4}$

A

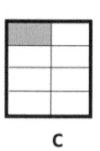 $= \frac{1}{8}$

C

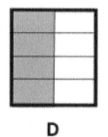 $= \frac{3}{4}$

B

$= \frac{4}{8}$

D

11. A pizza was divided into eighths. Helena ate $\frac{2}{8}$ of the pizza. Jeremy ate $\frac{3}{8}$ of the pizza. Frances ate $\frac{1}{8}$ of the pizza. How much of the pizza was left?

A $\frac{2}{3}$

B $\frac{1}{4}$

C $\frac{1}{2}$

D $\frac{1}{8}$

12. $\frac{3}{9} + \frac{2}{9} =$

    A $\frac{5}{9}$

    B $\frac{1}{9}$

    C $\frac{1}{3}$

    D $\frac{2}{3}$

13. What's the difference?

    $\frac{3}{6} - \frac{1}{6} =$

    A $\frac{2}{3}$

    B $\frac{1}{6}$

    C $\frac{5}{6}$

    D $\frac{1}{3}$

14. Julian has $7.00 to buy a baseball that costs $6.74. How much change should he get back?

    A $0.30

    B $0.28

    C $0.26

    D $0.24

15. Stewart bought these three things.

What was the total of these three items?

    A $6.55

    B $7.67

    C $9.13

    D $9.77

16. Christina bought 3 dolls for $9.39. How much did each doll cost to buy?

    A $1.12

    B $3.13

    C $18.78

    D $28.17

17. If each pen costs $2.12, how much must Yuki pay for four pens?

    A $1.12

    B $3.13

    C $8.48

    D $29.17

18. Martin shaded $\frac{3}{4}$ of the figure.

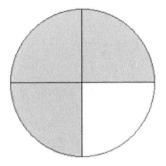

Which decimal equals $\frac{3}{4}$?

    A 75.0

    B 7.5

    C 0.75

    D 0.075

19. Which number is 7 more than 3014?

    A 3131

    B 3121

    C 3031

    D 3021

20. What is $408 - 193 =$

     A 315

     B 305

     C 215

     D 205

21. Kristen did this division problem.

$$360 \div 18 = 20$$

Which problem could she do to check her answer?

     A $20 \times 18 = \square$

     B $20 \div 18 = \square$

     C $20 + 18 = \square$

     D $20 - 18 = \square$

This space left blank intentionally

22. The figure below is a model for the multiplication sentence.

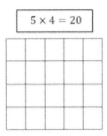

Which division sentence is modeled by the same figure?

     A $4 \div 2 = 2$

     B $20 \div 5 = 4$

     C $40 \div 5 = 8$

     D $80 \div 4 = 20$

23. How much is eight times nine hundred seventy-three?

     A 7254

     B 7384

     C 7654

     D 7784

24. There are 175 students making 5 cards for hospital patients. How many cards will they make all together?

     A 180

     B 525

     C 875

     D 955

25. A company has 17 small delivery trucks. Each truck has 6 wheels. How many wheels is this in all?

    A 96

    B 102

    C 108

    D 162

26. On a field trip at the museum there were 858 students that were equally divided from 6 different schools. How many students were from each school?

    A 143

    B 148

    C 152

    D 153

27. An ice cream shop has made 476 flyers to get more business. They plan on passing out the flyers at an equally divided rate at 7 different parking lots. How many flyers will they pass out at each parking lot?

    A 64

    B 68

    C 72

    D 76

28. Which number sentence is true?

    A $153 \div 1 = 153 \times 1$

    B $153 \div 153 = 153 \times 1$

    C $153 \div 153 = 153 \times 0$

    D $153 \div 153 = 153 \times 153$

29. What number can be multiplied with 2958 to give the answer 2958?

$$2958 \times \boxed{} = 2958$$

    A 4187

    B 100

    C 1

    D 0

30. Chase bought 8 toy cars. All the toy cars were the same price. The total cost was $56. How much money did each toy car cost?

    A $448

    B $56

    C $28

    D $7

This space left blank intentionally

31. Glenda has $40. She paid $20 for a pair of shoes. Then she went to a bookstore to buy a book for $6. What amount did Glenda have left?

    A $14

    B $16

    C $24

    D $26

32. In one week, a library checks out 1253 books on Wednesday and 1791 books on Friday. If the library checks out the same number of books for 2 weeks in a row, how many books will they checkout in all?

    A 3046

    B 4297

    C 4835

    D 6088

33. Mrs. Rogers bought 50 stickers for her class. She plans on giving an equal amount to each student, 2 stickers. Which number sentence could be used to find out how many students does she have in her class?

    A $50 \times 2 = \square$

    B $50 \div 2 = \square$

    C $50 + 2 = \square$

    D $50 - 2 = \square$

34. Dennis mowed a lawn and was paid $20 before the job began. After he mowed the lawn, he was given a $5 bonus. Which expression shows how much money did he receive in all for the job?

A $\$20 \times \$5 = \square$

B $\$20 \div \$5 = \square$

C $\$20 + \$5 = \square$

D $\$20 - \$5 = \square$

35. Which statement shows twice as much as 11?

A $2 + 11$

B $2 - 11$

C 2×11

D $2 \div 11$

36. Which expression shows 3 less than 15?

A $15 - 3$

B $15 + 3$

C $15 \div 3$

D 15×3

This space left blank intentionally

37. Which number makes this sentence true?

$$4 + 7 < 2 \times \square$$

    A 2

    B 3

    C 5

    D 6

38. Which sign goes in the box to make the number sentence true?

$$11 \; \square \; 4 = 7$$

    A +

    B −

    C ×

    D ÷

39. Which of the following is used to find how many feet are in 48 inches?

    A $48 \div 12$

    B 48×12

    C $48 - 12$

    D $48 + 12$

40. If $5 \times 12 \times 14 = 840$, then what is $12 \times 5 \times 14$?

    A 70

    B 168

    C 840

    D 4200

41. If pears are on sale for 2 for $0.75, how much will 4 pears cost?

    A $0.79

    B $1.50

    C $4.50

    D $6.00

42. If an eraser cost $0.15 each, how much will 5 cost?

    A $0.30

    B $0.45

    C $0.60

    D $0.75

43. The table shows the number of stickers given in a package.

Number of Packages	Number of Stickers
1	12
2	24
3	36

If each package has the same number of stickers in it, how many are in 6 packages?

   A 48

   B 60

   C 72

   D 84

44. Look at the linear pattern below.

$$5, 10, 15, 20, 25, 30, \_\_\_$$

What comes next in this pattern?

   A 25

   B 35

   C 40

   D 45

This space left blank intentionally

45. Which of the following objects can hold more than 2 gallons?

A soda can   B milk carton   C juice box   D bathtub

46. What is the area of this figure?

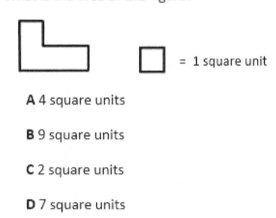   = 1 square unit

A 4 square units

B 9 square units

C 2 square units

D 7 square units

This space left blank intentionally

47. A rectangle is 8 inches long and 3 inches wide. What is the area of the rectangle?

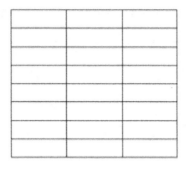

A 24 square inches

B 21 square inches

C 18 square inches

D 15 square inches

48. What is the perimeter of this figure?

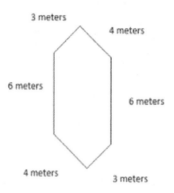

A 20 meters

B 22 meters

C 24 meters

D 26 meters

49. Each side of the pentagon is 5 inches long.

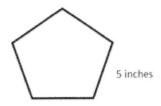

5 inches

What is the perimeter in inches of the pentagon?

    A 25 inches

    B 20 inches

    C 15 inches

    D 10 inches

50. A garden is shaped like a rectangle 12 feet long and 9 feet wide.

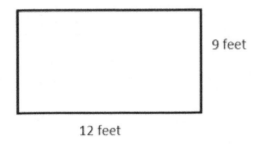

9 feet

12 feet

What is the perimeter in feet of the garden?

    A 46 feet

    B 42 feet

    C 38 feet

    D 108 feet

51. In 1 kilometer there are 1,000 meters. How many kilometers are in 10,000 meters?

    A 1,000 kilometers

    B 100 kilometers

    C 10 kilometers

    D 1 kilometer

52. Which sign is shaped like an octagon?

A

MAIN St.

C

B

YIELD

D

This space left blank intentionally

53. The figure below is what shape?

A circle

B triangle

C octagon

D pentagon

54. What figure is the shape below?

A rectangle

B hexagon

C oval

D pentagon

55. Which of these triangles shows a right angle?

A

C

B

D

56. How many right angles are in a square?

    A 0

    B 1

    C 2

    D 4

57. Which of these shapes does not always have a right angle?

    A square

    B rectangle

    C parallelogram

    D They all have right angles.

58. In the picture, which numbered angle measures MORE than a right angle?

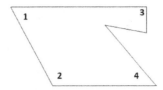

A 1

B 2

C 3

D 4

59. Which object is a cone?

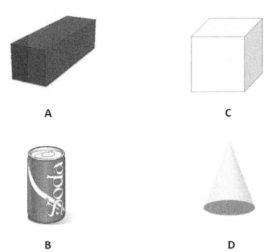

60. Which shapes make up this solid object?

    A rectangle and circle

    B cylinder and square solid

    C cone and cube

    D square, rectangle, and cylinder

61. There are 10 stickers in a bag. There are 1 green, 3 red, 2 yellow, and 4 blue stickers. What color is LEAST likely to be picked out of the bag next?

    A green

    B red

    C yellow

    D blue

This space left blank intentionally

62. A group of friends tossed a coin 13 times. The coin landed on heads 6 times and tails 7 times. Which tally chart shows these tosses?

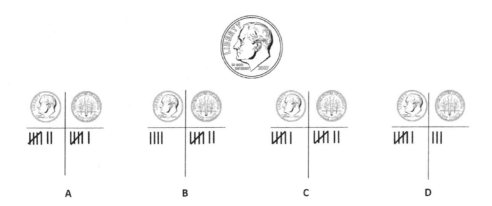

A   B   C   D

63. Luis asked his classmates to name their favorite recess activity. 10 classmates like playing tag, 7 classmates like hopscotch, and 5 classmates like climbing the monkey bars.

Which of the following charts show Luis' information?

Favorite Recess Activity

Tag	ЖII
Hopscotch	ЖII
Monkey Bars	ЖI

A

Favorite Recess Activity

Tag	ЖI
Hopscotch	Ж
Monkey Bars	ЖI

B

Favorite Recess Activity

Tag	Ж Ж
Hopscotch	Ж
Monkey Bars	Ж

C

Favorite Recess Activity

Tag	Ж Ж
Hopscotch	ЖII
Monkey Bars	Ж

D

64. A spinner landed on "Square" 4 times and "Circle" 7 times. Which tally chart shows these results?

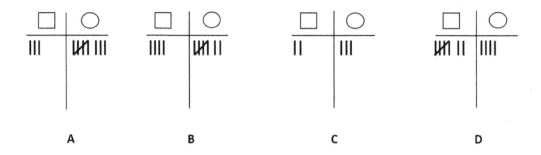

A   B   C   D

This space left blank intentionally

65. Shelly tossed 2 dimes 10 times. The results are shown in the tally chart below.

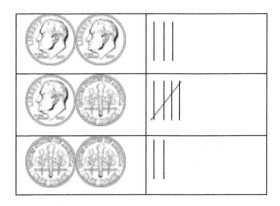

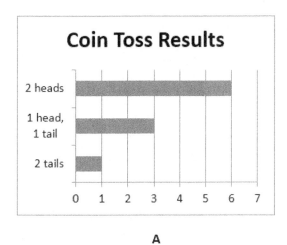

A

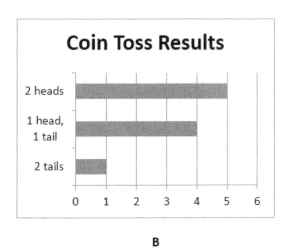

B

Coin Toss Results

C

Coin Toss Results

D

1.

D. 7102

In standard form, the number seven thousand one hundred two is written as 7102.

2.

B. seven thousand two hundred three

When writing the number 7203 in written form we would first write the thousands, then the hundreds and one's place. We would not need to mention the tens place since it is a zero.

The final written number would then be seven thousand two hundred three.

3.

A. 123, 132, 256, 281

The numbers in order from least to greatest (smallest to largest in number) are 123,132,256,281

4.

C. 1133

The number that has a three in both the tens and <u>ones</u> place is 1133.

5.

A. 7

The 7 represents the ones place, 7, in the number 3847.

6.

D. 904

The standard form of the written number nine hundred four is 904.

7.

A. 520

517 rounded to the nearest ten is 520 since we look at the number to the right of the tens, the ones place, to round the number. If the number is five or above, we round up to the next ten; if the number is four or below, we are rounding down staying on the same ten. Seven is closer to the next ten, therefore our number will be 520.

8.

C. $300 + 50 + 2$

The expanded notation of 352 is $300 + 50 + 2$.

9.

B. 7906

$7000 + 900 + 6$ is equal to 7906.

10.

A.

Rectangle $A\frac{2}{6}$ is the same as $\frac{1}{3}$ the original rectangle shown since both are equal to $\frac{1}{3}$.

11.

D. $\frac{1}{2}$

$\frac{2}{6} + \frac{1}{6}$ Is equal to $\frac{3}{6}$ which is equal to $\frac{1}{2}$.

12.

B. 1

To solve this problem, we first must add together all of the slices of cake ate. The slices ate were $\frac{3}{6} + \frac{1}{6} + \frac{2}{6}$, which is a total of $\frac{6}{6}$ of the cake ate. The fraction $\frac{6}{6}$ is equal to one whole, therefore 1 cake or whole cake was eaten.

13.

A. $\frac{1}{5}$

$\frac{4}{5} - \frac{3}{5} = \frac{1}{5}$ Since $4 - 3 = 1$.

14.

C. $0.65

To solve this problem, we must subtract $10.00 from $9.35 that requires borrowing since the bottom number is bigger than the top therefore, we must borrow from the left. We begin subtracting the ones place, ten minus five equals five. Next, we subtract the tens place nine minus three equals six. Finally, we subtract the hundreds place nine minus nine equals zero.

The cents we have left are sixty-five that can be written as $0.65.

15.

A. $5.43

To find the difference in price between Brand B and Brand A, we must subtract B from A: $19.99 − $14.56. We then subtract right to left, nine minus six equals three. Next, we move to the tens place, nine minus five equals four. Then we subtract the hundreds place (ones dollar amount), nine minus four is five. Finally, we can subtract the last number on the left, one minus one is zero.

Our answer would then be $5.43 leaving our decimal point between the dollars and cents.

16.

D. $1. 10

To find out how much each book cost, we must divide. $5.50 goes into 5 $1.10 times, which would be $1.10.

17.

C. $5. 00

To find out how much each child would receive, we must divide. $25.00 Goes into 5 500 times, which would be $5.00.

18.

B. 0. 5

The fraction $\frac{1}{2}$ is equal to the decimal 0.5.

19.

A. 57

The missing number for the problem $74 + \square = 131$ is 57 since $4 + 7 = 11$ for the ones then you carry your one ten over to the tens place and $1 + 7 + 5 = 13$. Putting the tens and ones together, you would get 131.

20.

C. 4998

To find the answer, we must add together the two numbers, 3707 and 1291. There is no carrying in this addition problem making it easier to add; $3707 + 1291 = 4998$.

21.

D. 18 ÷ 6 = 3

The division problem that is modeled by the same multiplication problem is $18 \div 6 = 3$ since all three numbers that were in the multiplication problem ($6 \times 3 = 18$).

22.

B. 84 ÷ 7 = 12

The number sentence that Oliver used that was different than Annie's but was the same problem is $84 \div 7 = 12$ since the problem Annie used was $12 \times 7 = 84$ and it is multiplication, the opposite of division but is using the same numbers making it the same problem.

23.

C. 1008

To solve the word problem, we must multiply the two numbers given since they will give us the total number of people that sit in the cafeteria during the four lunches served.

$$252 \times 4 = 1008$$

24.

A. 3948

To solve this problem, we must multiply 564 with 7 as shown: $564 \times 4 = 3948$.

25.

D. 4200

To solve the word problem, we must multiply the two numbers given since they will give us the total number of people that visited the park on Saturday.

$$1050 \times 4 = 4200$$

26.

B. 128

To solve this word problem, we must divide the smaller number, four, into the larger number, 512 to get our answer.

$$512 \div 4 = 128$$

27.

B. 1876

To solve this word problem, we must divide the smaller number, three, into the larger number, 5628 to get our answer.

$$5628 \div 3 = 1876$$

28.

D. 0

The number that needs to be multiplied with 4187 to equal 0is 0. When any number is multiplied with zero the answer to the problem, or the product, will be zero.

29.

C. $642 \div 1 = 642 \times 1$

The number sentence $642 \div 1 = 642 \times 1$ is true since both number sentences are both equal to 642. When any number is multiplied or divided by one it equals itself.

30.

D. $9

To solve this problem, we must divide the total amount of candles bought, 7 and divide into the total amount spent, $63 to get our answer of $9 spent for each candle.

31.

C. $11

To solve this word problem, we must subtract from our money twice. First, we must subtract the amount of the baseball cap $11 from the original amount Thomas has $30.

$$\$30 - \$11 = \$19$$

Now Thomas has $19 and is going to buy a ticket to the game for $8. We must subtract $8 from $19 to get our final answer.

$$\$19 - \$8 = \$11$$

Thomas will have left $11.

32.

B.5208

This is a multiple step word problem. To find our answer we must multiply each of the miles by 4 to get the number of miles over the 4 weeks. Then we must add the two numbers together to get total amount of miles.

First multiply each mileage by four.

$$704 \times 4 = 2816$$

$$598 \times 4 = 2392$$

Then add the two numbers together to get our answer.

$$2816 + 2392 = 5208$$

The total amount of miles driven is 5208.

33.

A. $36 \div 3 = \square$

To find the correct number sentence, we must first know what the word problem is asking us. It wants us to find the number of water bottles that are in each container. Since there are an equal number of bottles in each container, we can use division to create our number sentence. The number sentence would be $36 \div 3 = 12$.

34.

D. $\$5 - \$3.25 = \square$

To find the correct number sentence, we must know what the word problem is asking. Shauna bought a package of strawberries and we want to know how much money has been taken away from her original amount. If we are taking something <u>away</u> then our number sentence will involve subtraction. The number sentence would be $\$5 - \$3.25 = \$1.75$.

35.

B. $4 + 10$

The correct number sentence to use when the words more than are used in a word problem is an addition sentence.

36.

C. $12 \div 2$

The correct number sentence to use when using the words half of a number are used in a word problem, it is a division sentence.

37.

B. 4

The missing number in the number sentence is 4 since $5 + 7$ and 4×3 both equal 12.

38.

B. ×

The sign that goes in the number sentence $8 \;\boxed{}\; 4 = 32$ is a multiplication sign since $8 \times 4 = 32$ and none of the other signs given would give us this answer.

39.

D. 7 hours

To find out how many hours Francesca practiced we need to divide the total minutes into 60. $420 \div 60 = 7$ hours

40.

C. 360

The multiplication problem $4 \times 9 \times 10$ is equal to $9 \times 4 \times 10$ therefore they would have the answer of 360.

41.

B. $7.50

To find the answer to this word problem, we must multiply the cost of each bunch of grapes, $2.50 by the amount we want to get, 3.

$$\$2.50 \times 3 = \$7.50$$

The cost of 3 bunches of grapes is $7.50.

42.

B. $1.29

To find the cost of 2 oranges and 3 limes we first must multiply each amount of fruit by its price then we add together the two amounts of fruits.

$$2 \times \$0.33 = \$0.66$$

$$3 \times \$0.21 = \$0.63$$

$$\$0.66 + \$0.63 = \$1.29$$

The total amount of 2 oranges and 3 limes is $1.29.

43.

A. $1.16

To find the answer to this word problem we can either multiply the price of one, $0.29 by 4, or add $0.29 to the price of 3 markers, $0.87.

In this case, we will multiply $0.29 by 4.

$$\$0.29 \times 4 = \$1.16$$

Four markers will cost $1.16.

44.

B. 36

The linear pattern is counting by 6's. Therefore, the pattern would go after 30 to 36 since $30 + 6 = 36$.

45.

C. yards

The best way to measure a football field is by measuring it in yards.

46.

D. 7 square units

The area of the figure is 7 square units with 5 of the units on top and 2 of the units on the bottom.

47.

C. 35 square units

To find the area of the rectangle, we need to multiply the length by the width of the rectangle.

$$5 \times 7 = 35 \text{ Square units}$$

The area of the rectangle is 35 square units.

48.

B. 14 meters

To solve for perimeter, we must add all four of the sides together. We would add $4 + 4 + 3 + 3$ to solve our problem.

$$4 + 4 + 3 + 3 = 14$$

There is a total of 14 meters for the perimeter of the kitchen.

49.

A. 27 feet

To solve the perimeter of the polygon we must add all six sides together.

$$8 + 2 + 3 + 3 + 5 + 6 = 27$$

The total perimeter of the polygon is 27 feet.

50.

C. 24 inches

The total perimeter of the parallelogram is 24 inches since each side of the parallelogram is 6inches and there is a total of 4 sides and $6 + 6 + 6 + 6 = 24$ inches.

51.

C. 38

There is a total of 38 inches in 3 feet 2 inches. Each foot has a total of 12 inches in it. We can multiply 3 feet by 12 inches to get 36 inches.

$$3 \times 12 = 36$$

Then we can add on the additional 2 inches to get our answer of 38 inches.

$$36 + 2 = 38$$

52.

D.

Shape D is a pentagon. A pentagon has 5 sides and shape D is the only shape given out of the choices that show a shape with 5 sides.

53.

B. hexagon

The shape that was shown is a hexagon. A hexagon is a shape that has 6 sides. The figure that was drawn has 6 sides and would be considered a hexagon.

54.

B.

Shape B is an octagon. An octagon is an 8-sided shape. Shape B is the only answer shape drawn that has 8 sides.

55.

A. 3 sides that are the same length.

An equilateral triangle is a triangle that has three equal sides to it or 3 sides that are the same length.

56.

C. 2

A parallelogram has 2 parallel sides to it.

57.

D. rectangle

A rectangle has 4 right angles, the other answer choices do not.

58.

B. 2

Angle 2 is the only right angle in the shape drawn. An angle must be 90^0 for it to be a right angle.

59.

A.

Picture A of the ball is an example of a sphere.

60.

C. cube and cylinder

The shapes that make up the solid object is a cube on left and a cylinder on the right.

61.

D. yellow

Out of the 14 marbles, most of the marbles, 7 of them, are yellow. Therefore, the most likely color to be picked out of the bag is yellow.

62.

B.

Chart B shows the correct number of tallies on the chart with 5 yellow, 2 blue, and 6 green.

63.

A.

Chart A shows the correct tallies and information that Simon collected with 2 tallies for sausage, 10 tallies for pepperoni, and 11 tallies for cheese.

64.

D.

Chart D shows the correct tally marks for each coin toss, 7 for heads and 5 for tails.

65.

B.

Graph B shows the correct number of tallies for the coin flips with Alan at 5, Jennifer at 3, and Nicholas at 7.

1.

A. 5087

In standard form, the number five thousand, eighty-seven is written as 5087.

2.

C. five thousand fifty-three

When writing the number 5053 in written form we would first write the thousands, then the tens and ones place. We would not need to mention the hundreds place since it is a zero.

The final written number would then be five thousand fifty-three.

3.

D. 293, 217, 154, 145

The numbers in order from greatest to smallest (the largest number to the smallest) is 293,217,154,145.

4.

B. 7742

The number that has a 7 in the thousands place and a 7 in the hundreds place is 7742.

5.

C. 5

The number that is in the tens place of 9851 is 5.

6.

D. 1015

The number that has the same digit in the thousands and tens place is 1015.

7.

B. 2100

The number 2129 rounded to the nearest hundred would be 2100 since the tens place is below four and would remain at the same hundreds place it is at.

8.

A. $100 + 40 + 3$

The expanded notation of 143 is $100 + 40 + 3$.

9.

C. 2018

$2000 + 10 + 8$ means the number 2018.

10.

D.

Square D of $\frac{4}{8}$ is equal to the original square of $\frac{1}{2}$ since both are the fraction of $\frac{1}{2}$.

11.

B. $\frac{1}{4}$

To solve this problem, we first must add together all of the slices of pizza ate. The slices ate were $\frac{2}{8} + \frac{3}{8} + \frac{1}{8}$, which is a total of $\frac{6}{8}$ of the pizza ate. Now we can subtract the total amount ate from the total pizza there is, $\frac{8}{8} - \frac{6}{8} = \frac{2}{8}$. The fraction $\frac{2}{8}$ is equal to $\frac{1}{4}$.

12.

A. $\frac{5}{9}$

$\frac{3}{9} + \frac{2}{9} = \frac{5}{9}$ since $3 + 2 = 5$.

13.

D. $\frac{1}{3}$

$\frac{3}{6} - \frac{1}{6}$ is equal to $\frac{2}{6}$ which is equal to $\frac{1}{3}$.

14.

C. $0.26

To solve this problem, we must subtract $7.00 from $6.74 that requires borrowing since the bottom number is bigger than the top therefore, we must borrow from the left. We begin subtracting the ones place, ten minus four equals six. Next, we subtract the tens place nine minus seven equals two. Finally, we subtract the hundreds place six minus six equals zero.

The cents we have left are twenty-six that can be written as $0.26.

15.

D. $9.77

To find the solution for this problem, we must add together the cost of the toys that Stewart bought.

The three toys cost $2.10, $3.22 and $4.45.

16.

B. $3. 13

To find out how much each doll cost, we must divide. $9.39 Goes into 3 313 times, which would be $3.13.

17.

C. $8. 48

To determine the price of four pens, we must multiply the price of the pens by four, the number of pens bought. $2.12 × 4 = $8.48.

18.

C. 0. 75

The fraction $\frac{3}{4}$ is equal to the decimal 0.75.

19.

D. 3021

$3014 + 7 = 3021$ since $14 + 7 = 21$. The only place values that change in this problem would be the ones and tens place, the hundreds and thousands place would remain the same.

20.

C. 215

The problem $408 - 193$ can be solved by subtracting the ones first, followed by borrowing for the tens place from the hundreds place, subtracting the tens place and finally subtracting the hundreds place.

The ones place is eight minus three which is five.

The tens place we need to borrow since the bottom number is bigger than the top therefore, we must borrow from the left (from the hundreds place). The four hundreds becomes three after we borrow, and the tens become ten tens making it possible for us to subtract the nine tens at the bottom. Ten minus nine equals one.

The hundreds place is three minus one which is two.

21.

A. $20 \times 18 = \boxed{}$

To check Kristen's division problem, we need to do a multiplication problem since the opposite of division is multiplication. The multiplication problem would be $20 \times 18 = \boxed{}$

22.

B. $20 \div 5 = 4$

The division problem that is modeled by the same multiplication problem is $20 \div 5 = 4$ since all three numbers that were in the multiplication problem ($5 \times 4 = 20$).

23.

D. 7784

To solve this problem, we must multiply 973 with 8 as shown: $973 \times 8 = 7784$.

24.

C. 875

To solve the word problem, we must multiply the two numbers given since they will give us the total number of cards made by the students.

$$175 \times 5 = 875$$

25.

B. 102

To solve the word problem, we must multiply the two numbers given since they will give us the total number of wheels on the small delivery trucks.

$$17 \times 6 = 102$$

26.

A. 143

To solve this word problem, we must divide the smaller number, six, into the larger number, 858 to get our answer for how many students were from each school on the field trip.

$$858 \div 6 = 143$$

27.

B. 68

To solve this word problem, we must divide the smaller number, seven, into the larger number, 476 to get our answer.

$$476 \div 4 = 68$$

28.

A. $153 \div 1 = 153 \times 1$

The number sentence $153 \div 1 = 153 \times 1$ is true since both number sentences are both equal to 153.

29.

C. 1

The number that needs to be multiplied with 2958 to equal 2958 is 1. When any number is multiplied with one the answer to the problem, or the product, will be itself.

30.

D. $7

To solve this problem, we must divide the total amount of toy cars bought, 8 and divide into the total amount spent, $56 to get our answer of $7 spent for each toy car.

31.

A. $14

To solve this word problem, we must subtract from our money twice. First, we must subtract the amount of the pair of shoes $20 from the original amount Glenda has $40.

$$\$40 - \$20 = \$20$$

Now, Glenda has $20 and is going to buy a book from the bookstore for $6. We must subtract $6 from $20 to get our final answer.

$$\$20 - \$6 = \$14$$

Glenda will have left $14.

This space left blank intentionally

32.

d. 6088

This is a multiple step word problem. To find our answer we must multiply each of the books checked out by two to get the number of books checked out over the two weeks. Then we must add the two numbers together to get total amount of books checked out.

First multiply each by two.

$$1253 \times 2 = 2506$$

$$1791 \times 2 = 3582$$

Then add the two numbers together to get our answer.

$$2506 + 3582 = 6088$$

The total amount of books checked out is 6088.

33.

B. $50 \div 2 = \square$

To find the correct number sentence, we must first know what the word problem is asking us. It wants us to find the students that are in Mrs. Rogers' class. Since each student is getting an equal number of stickers out of the total stickers purchased, we can use division to create our number sentence. The number sentence would be $50 \div 2 = 25$.

34.

C. $\$20 + \$5 = \square$

To find the correct number sentence, we first must know what the word problem is asking us. Dennis was paid $20 for mowing the lawn and then given a $5 bonus. The problem wants to know how much money he made in all. This means it is an addition problem with our number sentence being $\$20 + \$5 = \$25$.

35.

C. 2×11

The correct number sentence to use when the words twice as much is used in a word problem is a multiplication sentence.

36.

A. 15 − 3

The correct number sentence to use when the words less than are used in a word problem it is a subtraction sentence.

37.

D. 6

The correct number that goes into the number sentence $4 + 7 < 2 \times \boxed{}$ is 6 since $4 + 7 = 11$ and $2 \times 6 = 12$. Eleven is less than twelve making the number sentence true.

38.

B. −

The sign that goes in the number sentence $11 \boxed{} 4 = 7$ is a division sign. This is the only sign choice that could work out of the signs given.

39.

A. 48 ÷ 12

To find the equation that would find how many feet are in 48 inches, we first must know how many inches are in one foot. There are 12 inches in one foot, this would cause us to divide to find the number of feet in 48 inches since division would be the only method out of the four answers given that would give us the correct answer. $48 \div 12 = 4$ feet

40.

C. 840

The multiplication problem $5 \times 12 \times 14$ is equal to $12 \times 5 \times 14$ therefore they would have the answer of 840.

41.

B. $1.50

To find the price of four pears, we must first remember that two pears cost seventy-five cents. We would only be doubling the seventy-five cents to buy four pears.

To solve we can either multiply seventy-five cents by two or add seventy-five cents with seventy-five cents. In this case, we will multiply.

$$\$0.75 \times 2 = \$1.50$$

42.

d. $0.75

To find the cost of 5 erasers, we must multiply the number of erasers with the cost of each eraser $0.15.

$$5 \times \$0.15 = \$0.75$$

The total cost of 5 erasers is $0.75.

43.

C. 72

To find out how many stickers are in 6 packages we must multiply the number of stickers in each package, 12 by 6.

$$12 \times 6 = 72$$

There would be 72 stickers in 6 packages.

44.

B. 35

The linear pattern is counting by 5's. Therefore, the pattern would go after 30 to 35 since $30 + 5 = 35$.

45.

D. bathtub

The object that can hold more than 2 gallons is the bathtub. All other objects cannot hold more than 2 gallons of liquid.

46.

A. 4 square units

The area of the figure is 4 square units with 1 of the units on top and 3 of the units on the bottom.

47.

A. 24 square units

To find the area of the rectangle, we need to multiply the length by the width of the rectangle.

$$8 \times 3 = 24 \text{ Square units}$$

The area of the rectangle is 24 square units.

48.

D. 26 meters

To find the perimeter of an object, we must add all the sides together.

$$3 + 3 + 4 + 4 + 6 + 6 = 26$$

The total perimeter of the figure is 26 meters.

49.

A. 25 inches

The total perimeter of the pentagon is 25 inches since each side of the pentagon is 5 inches and there is a total of 5 sides and $5 + 5 + 5 + 5 + 5 = 25$ inches.

50.

B. 42 feet

To solve for perimeter, we must add all four of the sides together. We would add $12 + 12 + 9 + 9$ to solve our problem.

$$12 + 12 + 9 + 9 = 42$$

There is a total of 42 feet for the perimeter of the garden.

51.

C. 10 kilometers

If there are 10,000 meters, then that would equal 10 kilometers since 1 kilometer = 1,000 meters.

52.

A.

The stop sign, shape A, is an octagon. An octagon is a shape with 8 sides. The stop sign is the only sign shown that has 8 sides to it.

53.

D. pentagon

The figure that was shown is the pentagon shape. A pentagon is a 5-sided shape.

54.

B. hexagon

The figure drawn is a hexagon. A hexagon has 6 sides. The figure drawn has 6 sides total making it a hexagon.

55.

A.

Triangle A shows a right angle. The other triangles shown are isosceles and equilateral.

56.

D. 4

A square has 4 right angles since the shape has 4 equal sides.

57.

C. parallelogram

While a square and rectangle have 4 right angles, a parallelogram does not (in all cases). A parallelogram has parallel sides and opposite angles. Square and rectangles are parallelograms, but all parallelograms are not squares or rectangles.

58.

B. 2

Angle 2 is more than 90^0 (an obtuse angle) while angles 1 and 4 less than 90^0 (an acute angle), and angle 3 is a right angle.

59.

D.

Picture D is in the shape of a cone.

60.

B. cylinder and square solid

The shapes that make up the solid object is a cylinder on a left and a square solid on the right.

61.

A. green

Out of the 10 stickers, the least number of stickers, 1 of them, is green. Therefore, the least likely color to be picked out of the bag is green.

62.

C.

Tally chart C shows the correct amount of tally marks with 6 under heads and 7 under tails.

63.

D.

Chart D shows the correct tallies from Luis' information with 10 tallies for playing tag, 7 tallies for hopscotch, and 5 tallies for climbing monkey bars.

64.

B.

Chart B shows the correct number of tallies for each shape spun, 4 tallies for square and 7 tallies for circle.

65.

D.

Graph D shows the correct amount on each bar from the tally chart results with 3 for 2 heads, 5 for 1 head, 1 tail, and 2 for 2 tails.

Made in the USA
Las Vegas, NV
01 October 2022